COME FROM AWAY

ISBN 978-1-5400-0698-1

THE MUSICAL COMPANY

Exclusively Distributed By

HAL•LEONARD®

7777 W. BLUEMOUND RD. P.O. BOX 13819 MILWAUKEE, WI 53213

In Australia Contact:
Hal Leonard Australia Pty. Ltd.
4 Lentara Court
Cheltenham, Victoria, 3192 Australia
Email: ausadmin@halleonard.com.au

Visit Hal Leonard Online at
www.halleonard.com

WELCOME TO THE ROCK

Music and Lyrics by
IRENE SANKOFF
and DAVID HEIN

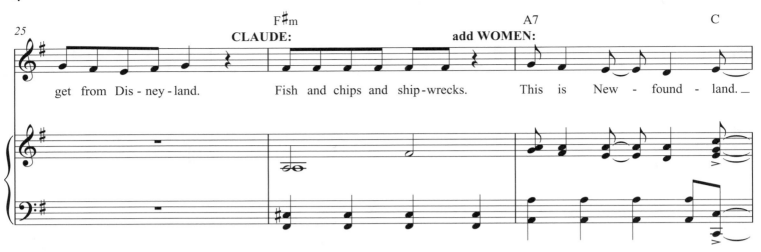

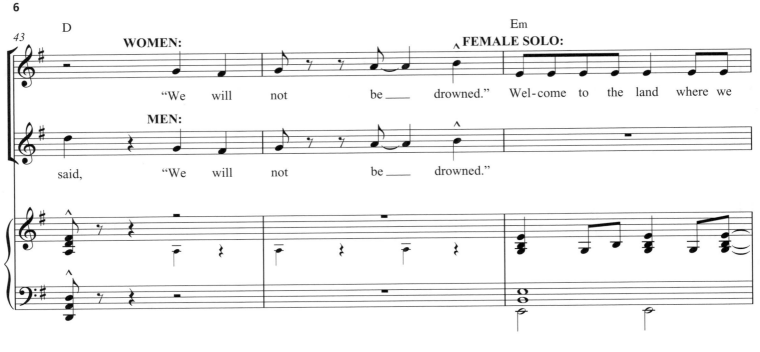

ev-er's in be-tween. To the ones who've left, you're nev-er tru-ly gone, a

WOMEN:

When the can-dle's in the win-dow and the ket-tle's al-ways on. When the

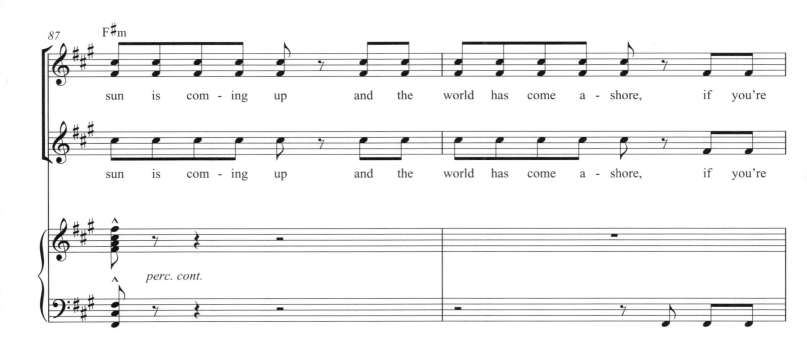

sun is com-ing up and the world has come a-shore, if you're

sun is com-ing up and the world has come a-shore, if you're

perc. cont.

BLANKETS AND BEDDING

Music and Lyrics by
IRENE SANKOFF
and DAVID HEIN

BEULAH: Crys-tal, I saw on the news that they're look-ing for blan-kets and bed-ding and may-be some food. Do you

CRYSTAL: know what they need and how much? I need some-thing to do, 'cause I can't watch the news an-y-more. Can I

MARTHA: | **ALL 3:** | **ANNETTE:**

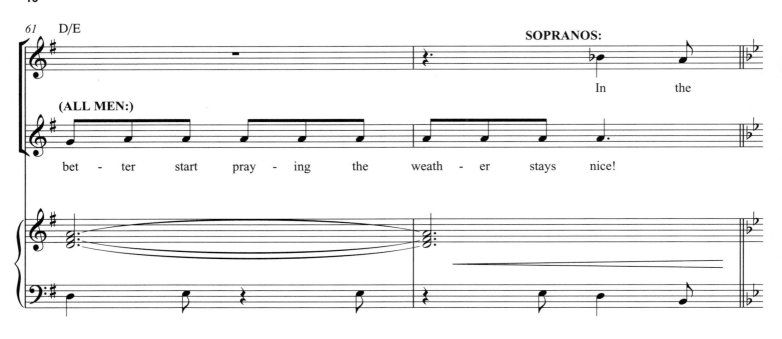

28 HOURS/WHEREVER WE ARE

Music and Lyrics by
IRENE SANKOFF
and DAVID HEIN

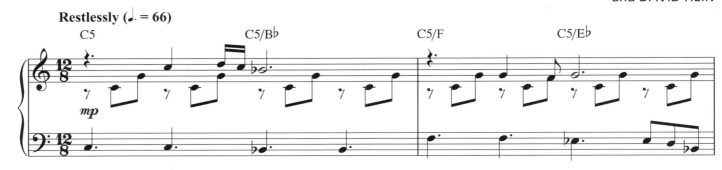

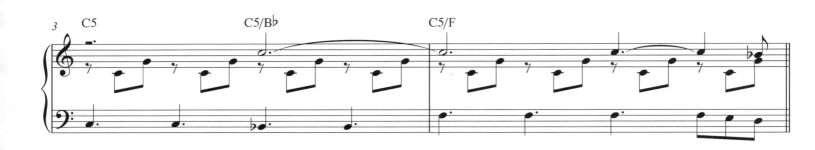

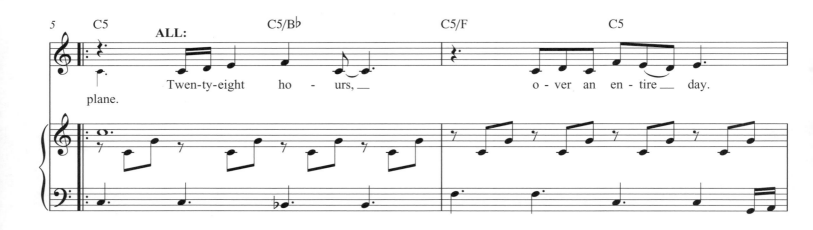

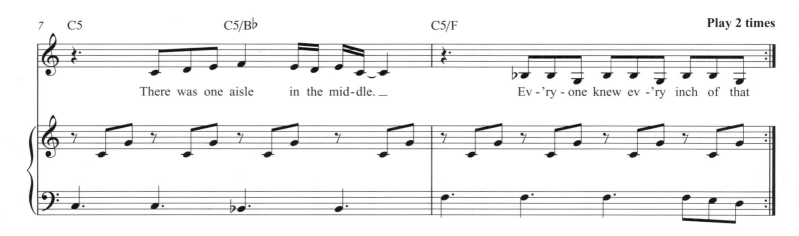

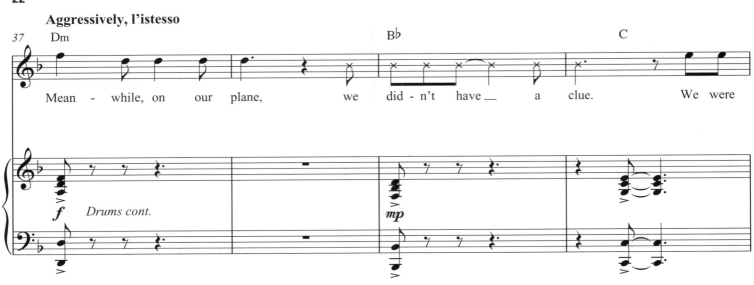

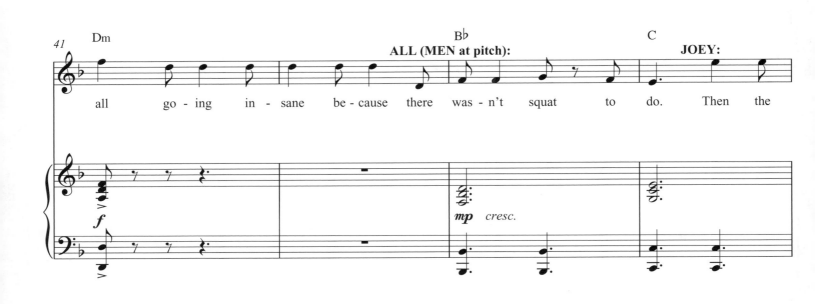

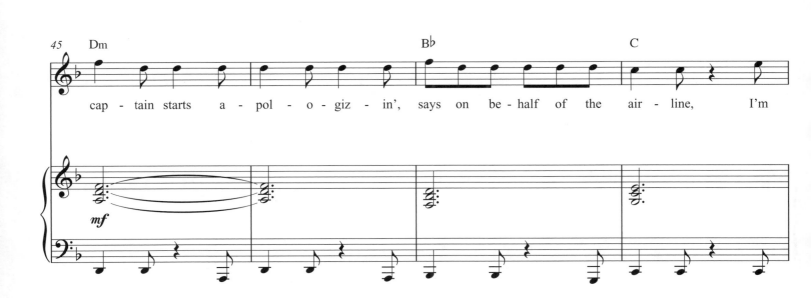

are.

are.

So the

flight at - tend - ants brought out all the min - i bot - tles of liq - uor and de -

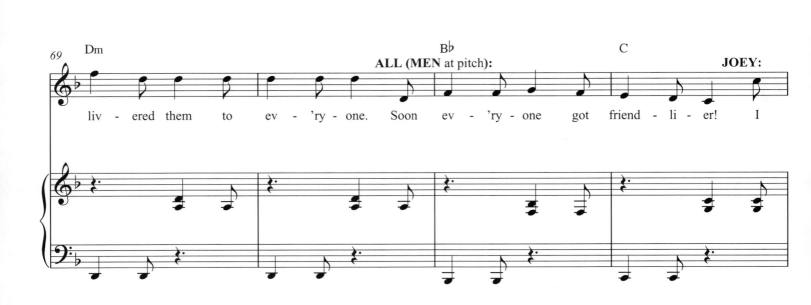

liv - ered them to ev - 'ry - one. Soon ev - 'ry - one got friend - li - er! I

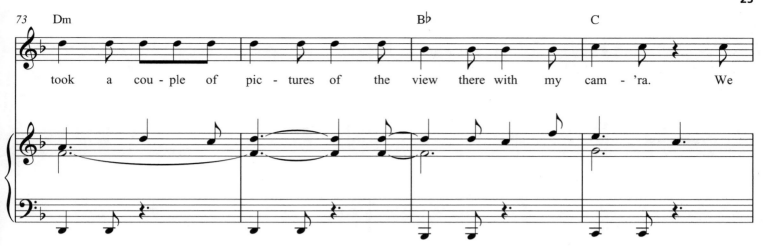

took a cou - ple of pic - tures of the view there with my cam - 'ra. We

add WOMEN:
did - n't know where we were, but we knew ___ that we were ham - mered! O - pen the

MEN:
but we knew ___ that we were ham - mered! O - pen the

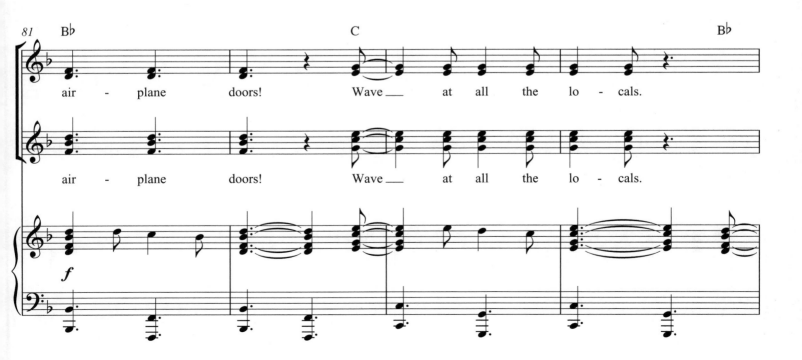

air - plane doors! Wave ___ at all the lo - cals.

air - plane doors! Wave ___ at all the lo - cals.

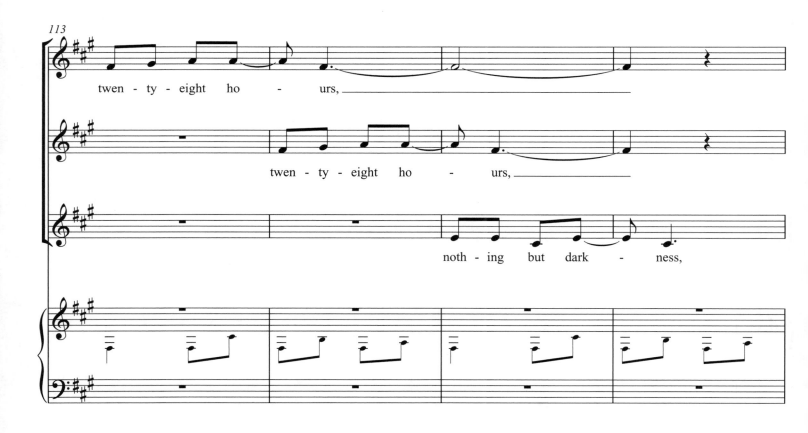

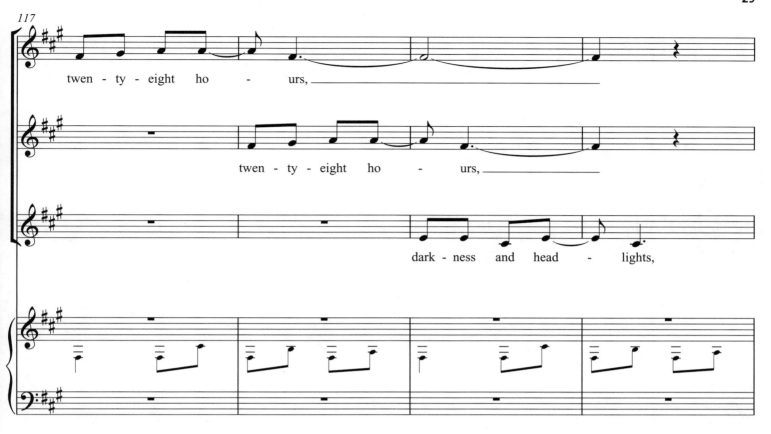

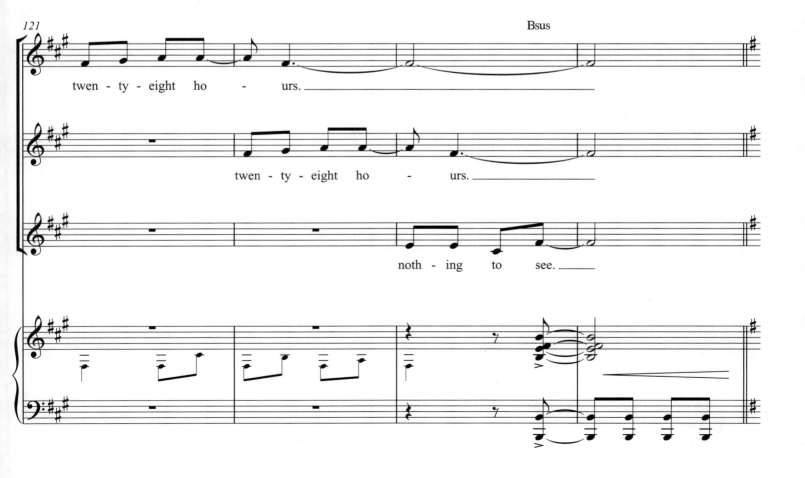

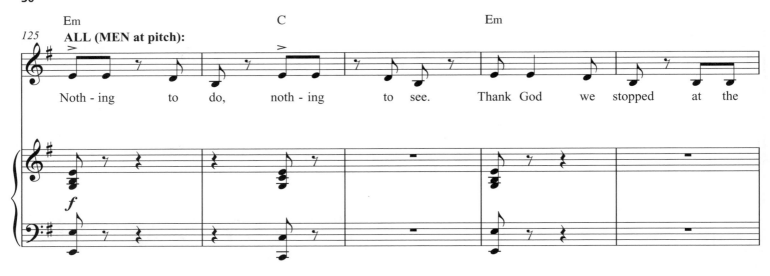

Noth - ing to do, noth - ing to see. Thank God we stopped at the

du - ty free. _____ Wher - ev - er we

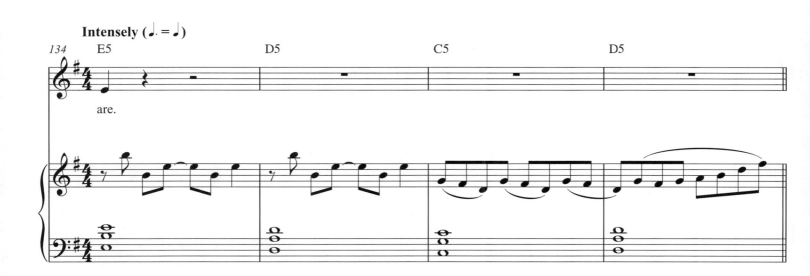

are.

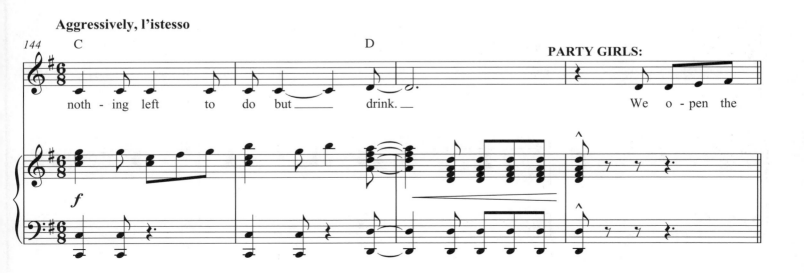

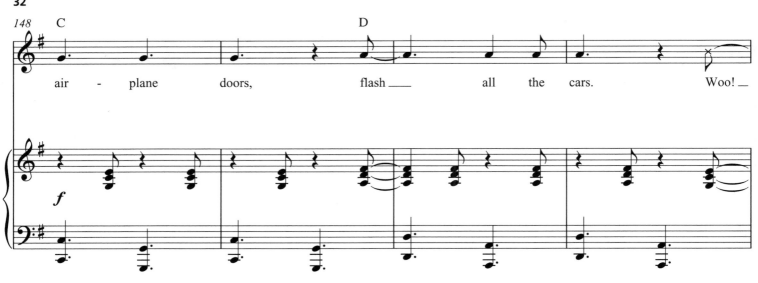

air - plane doors, flash ___ all the cars. Woo! ___

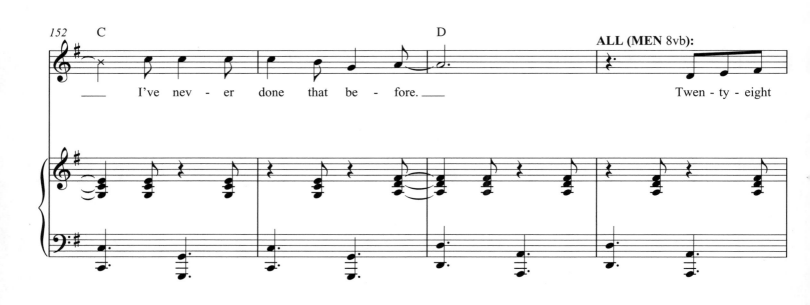

___ I've nev - er done that be - fore. ___ **ALL (MEN** 8vb)**:** Twen - ty - eight

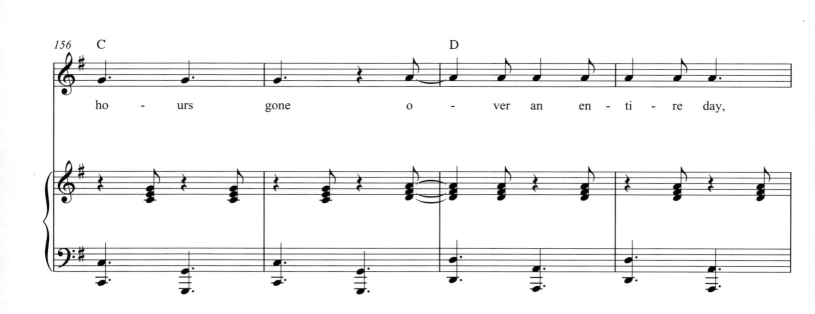

ho - urs gone o - ver an en - ti - re day,

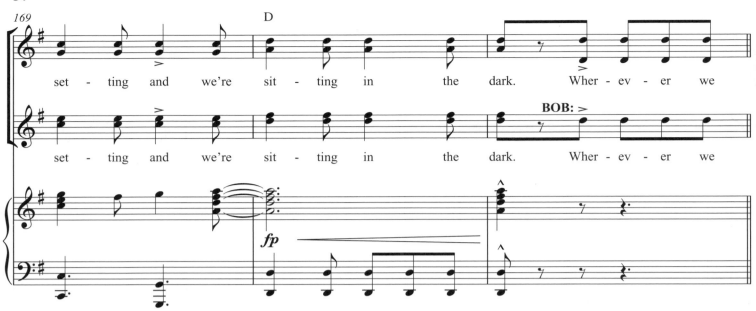

set - ting and we're sit - ting in the dark. Wher - ev - er we

set - ting and we're sit - ting in the dark. **BOB:** Wher - ev - er we

Slower, with freedom

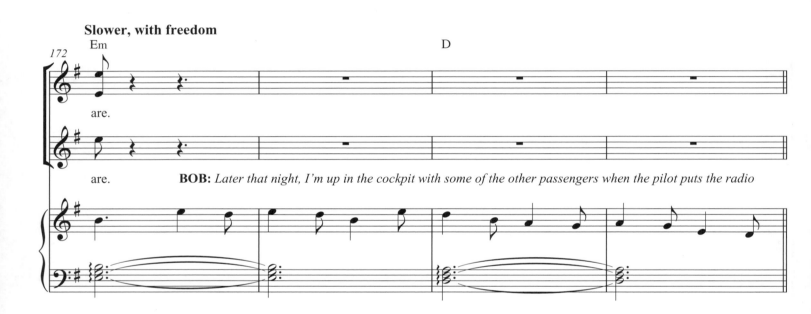

are.

are. **BOB:** *Later that night, I'm up in the cockpit with some of the other passengers when the pilot puts the radio*

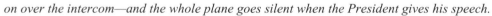

on over the intercom—and the whole plane goes silent when the President gives his speech.

Delicately (♩. = 66)

PRESIDENT BUSH: *I ask the American people to join me in saying a thanks for all the folks who have been fighting hard*

to rescue our fellow citizens and to join me in saying a prayer for the victims and their families. The resolve of our great nation

is being tested. But make no mistake: we will show the world that we will pass this test. God bless.

BEVERLEY: You got through to the air-line. Tom, I'm o-kay. Tell me what's hap-p'ning out there. How

bad is it? Tell me ev-'ry-thing, Tom. Who was __ in the air?

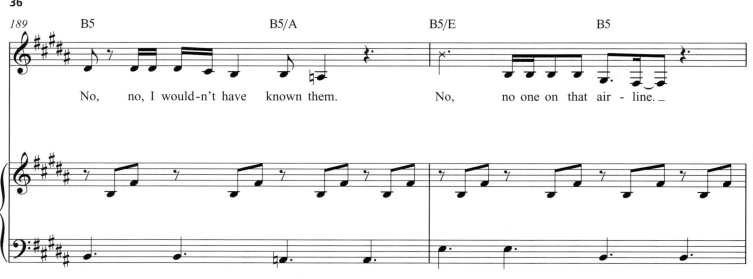

COSTUME PARTY

Music and Lyrics by
IRENE SANKOFF
and DAVID HEIN

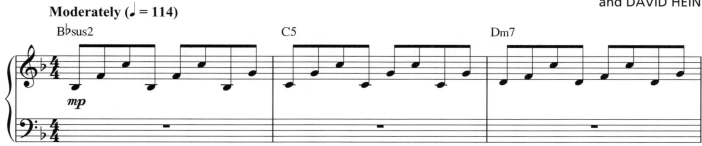

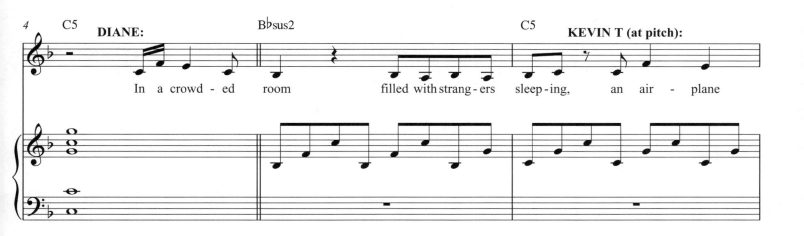

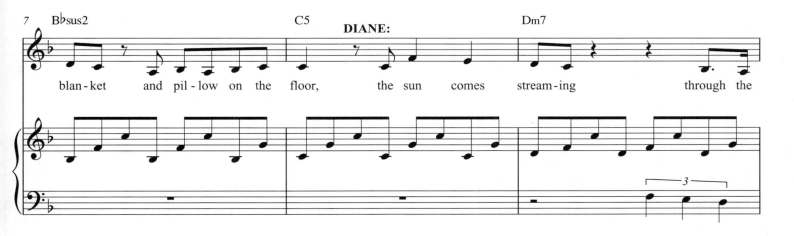

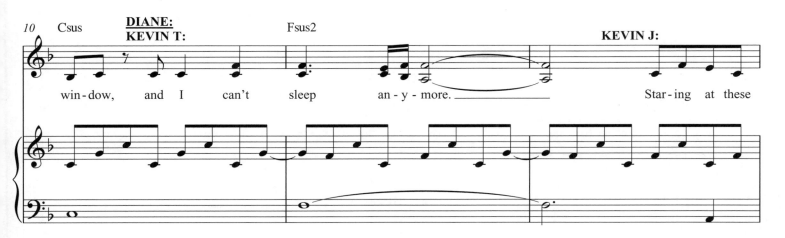

13 Bbsus2 ... C5 ... HANNAH: ... Bbsus2

strang-ers wak-ing up a-round me, sit-ting in a crowd of peo-ple wait-ing for the

16 C5 ... KEVIN J: ... Dm7

phone. And in a town ___ that's sud-den-ly dou-bled pop-u-

18 C5 ... HANNAH: DIANE: ... Fsus2

la-tion, I feel so a-lone. ___

KEVIN T: KEVIN J: ... KEVIN J:

I feel so a-lone. ___ It's like

21 Bb ... C ... KEVIN T: ... F ... C/E

an-y of us could have died on Tues-day, and like we're dared to see things dif-f'rent-ly ___ to-day.

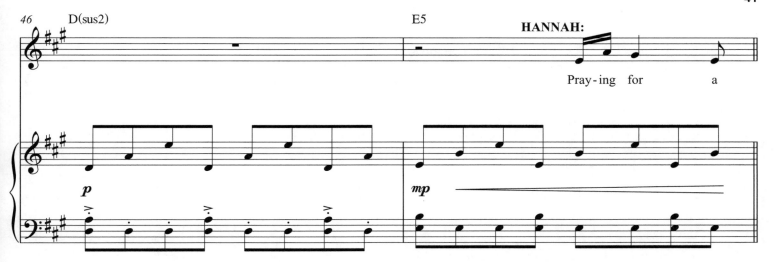

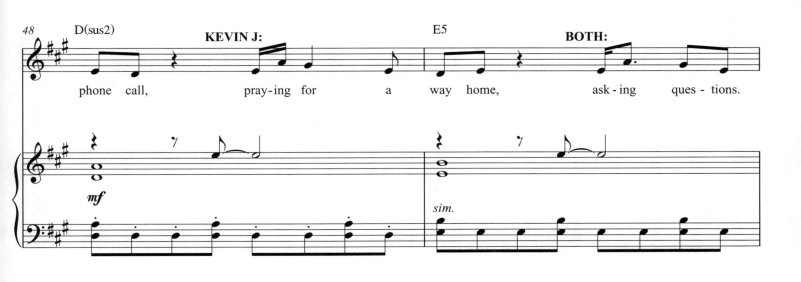

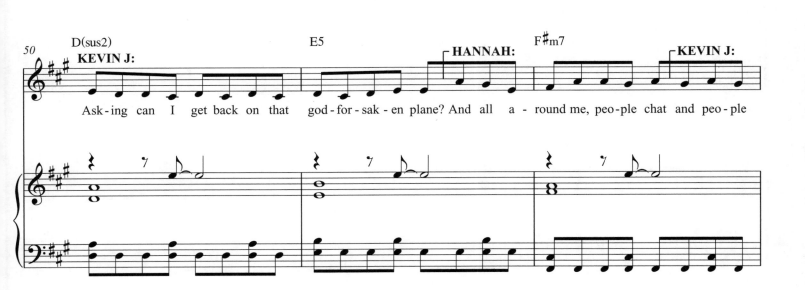

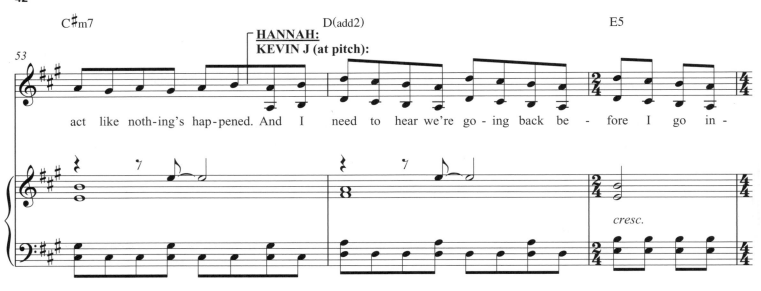

C#m7   D(add2)   E5

HANNAH:
KEVIN J (at pitch):

act like noth-ing's hap-pened. And I need to hear we're go-ing back be - fore I go in -

A5   A5/G

sane.

BEVERLEY: *Good morning. I'm Captain Beverley Bass. Now I know this is going to be hard to hear, but the American airspace remains closed. I can't tell you how long we'll be on the ground.*

mp sub.

A5/F   Em

DIANE:

But we are going to be here for some time.   Here for some time.

KEVIN J:

Here for some time.

cresc. poco a poco

I AM HERE

Music and Lyrics by
IRENE SANKOFF
and DAVID HEIN

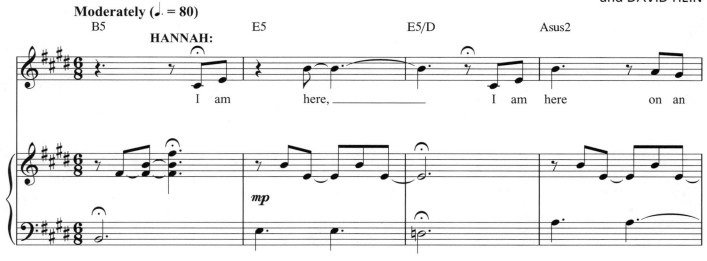

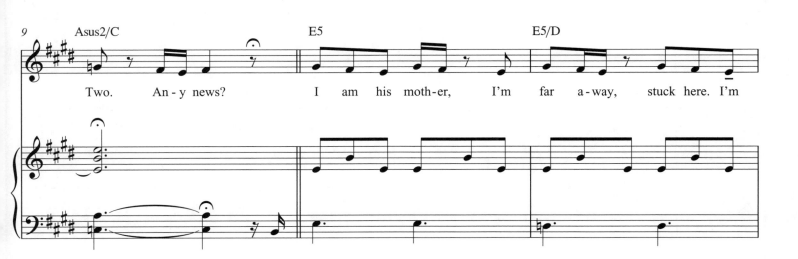

12 Asus2 — try-ing to find out if... Fine. I'll hold a-gain. E5 I should be down there and

colla voce *cresc.*

15 E5/D check-ing the hos-pi-tals, Asus2 put-ting up signs, do-ing some-thing! In-stead, I am Asus2/G

mf

18 E5 here, E5/D I am here Asus2 in Can-a-da. I am

8va

22 E5/G tell-ing you, list-en. My son, he takes risks. He's not miss-ing, he's help-ing or E5/F♯

cresc. poco a poco

PRAYER

Music and Lyrics by
IRENE SANKOFF
and DAVID HEIN

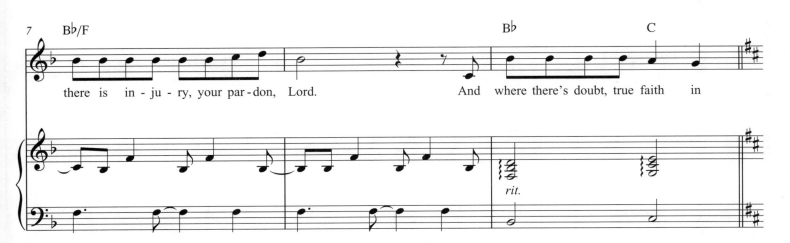

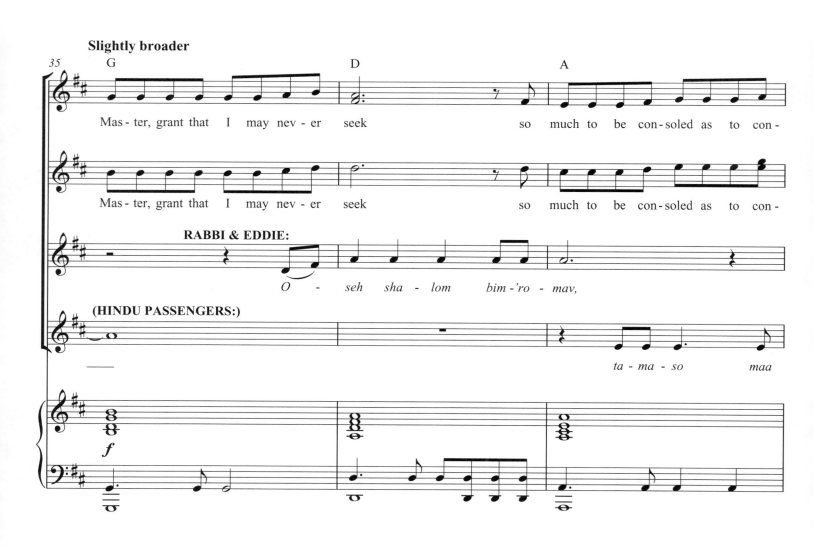

SCREECH IN

Music and Lyrics by
IRENE SANKOFF
and DAVID HEIN

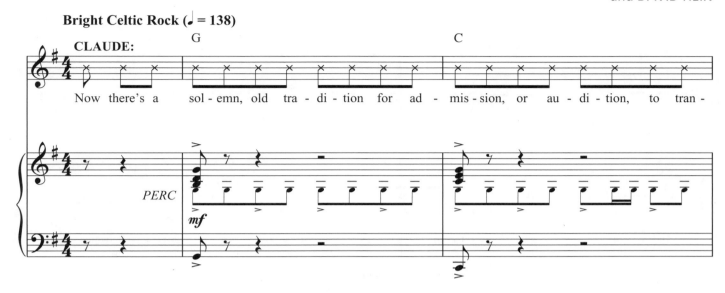

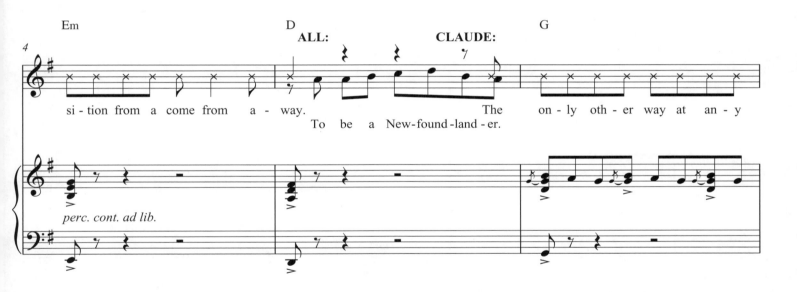

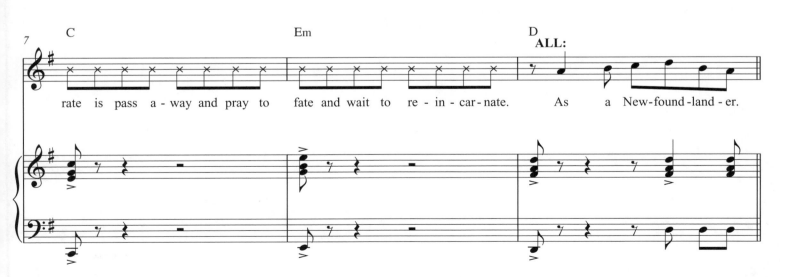

ME AND THE SKY

Music and Lyrics by
IRENE SANKOFF
and DAVID HEIN

Driving Folk Rock (♩ = 136)

the first fe - male A - mer - i - can cap - tain in his - to - ry.

Driving

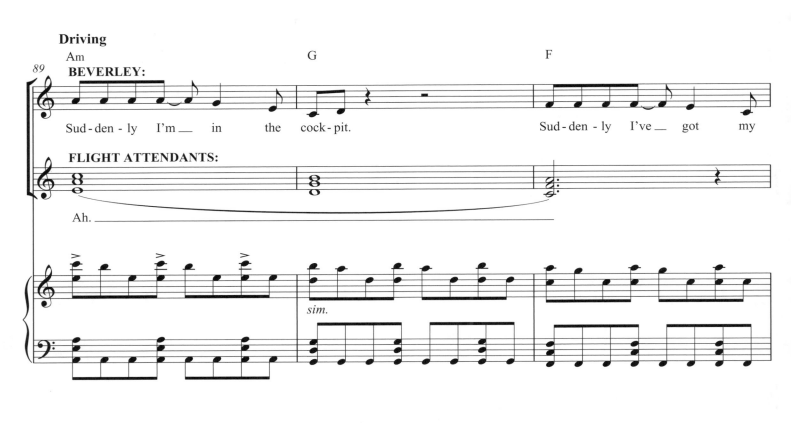

BEVERLEY:
Sud - den - ly I'm __ in the cock - pit. Sud - den - ly I've __ got my

FLIGHT ATTENDANTS:
Ah. _____

wings. Sud - den - ly all __ of those pi - lots pro - test - ing me,

Ah. _____

Sud-den-ly I've got __ an all fe - male __ crew. The news caught, and made

head-lines a - cross the world. Sud-den-ly it stopped: no one's say-in' you can't,

FLIGHT ATTENDANTS:

You can't,

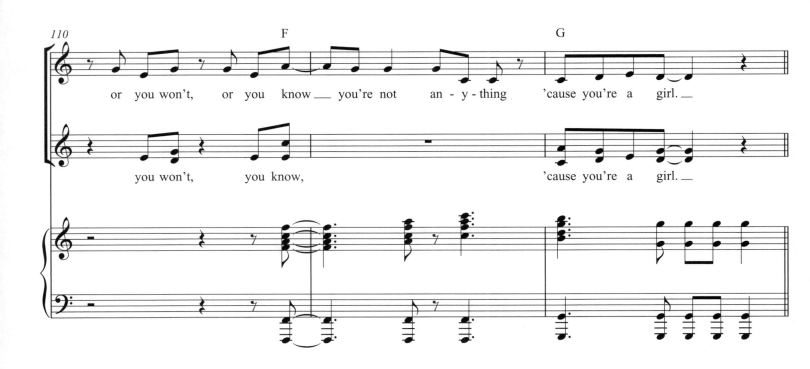

or you won't, or you know __ you're not an - y - thing 'cause you're a girl. __

you won't, you know, 'cause you're a girl. __

STOP THE WORLD

Music and Lyrics by
IRENE SANKOFF
and DAVID HEIN

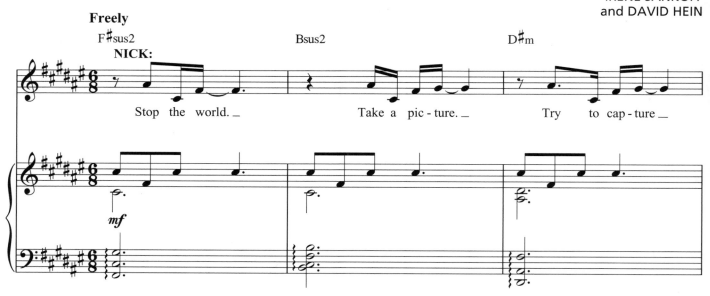

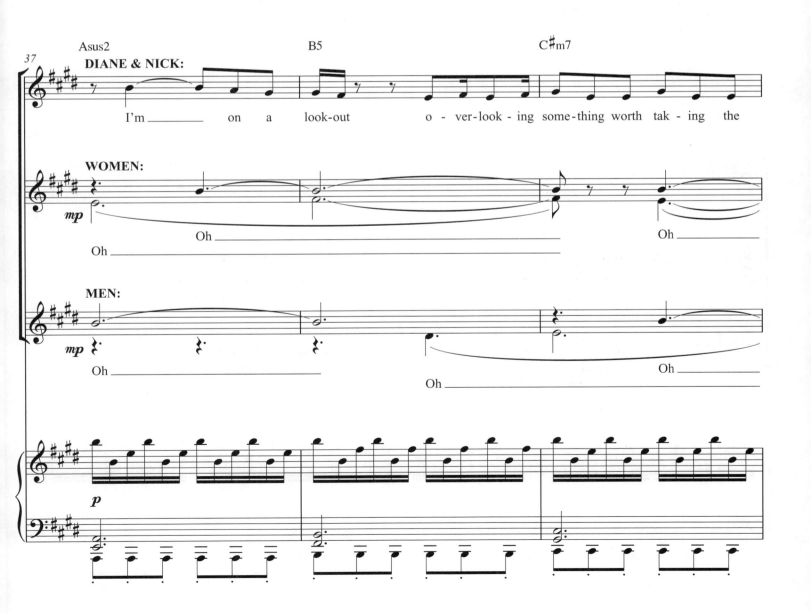

SOMEWHERE IN THE MIDDLE OF NOWHERE

Music and Lyrics by
IRENE SANKOFF
and DAVID HEIN

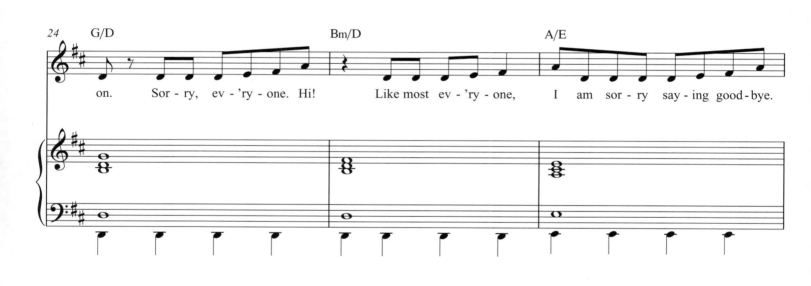

and I'm pass-ing a hat for the peo-ple who gave___ up their time, and they gave___

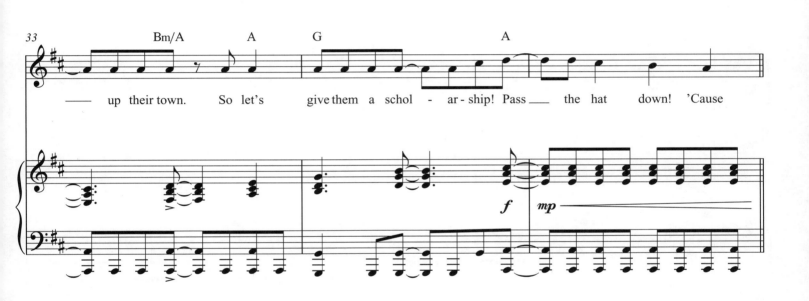

___ up their town. So let's give them a schol - ar-ship! Pass___ the hat down! 'Cause

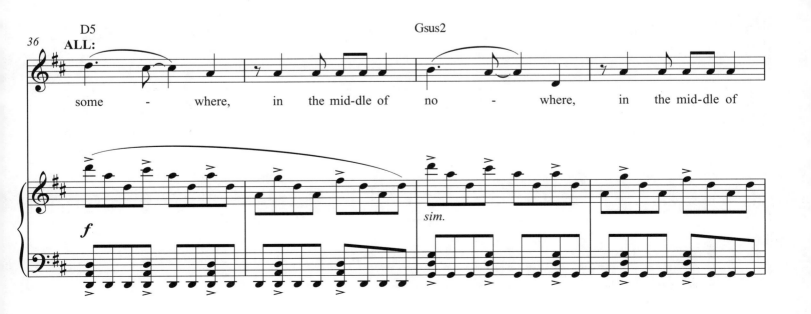

ALL:
some - where, in the mid-dle of no - where, in the mid-dle of

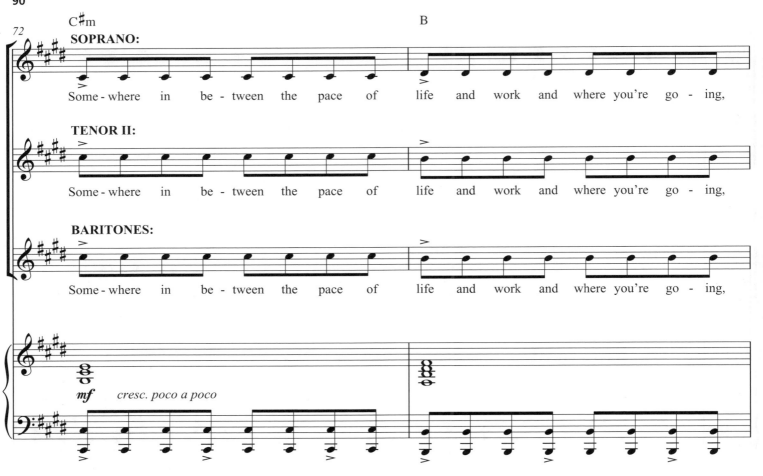

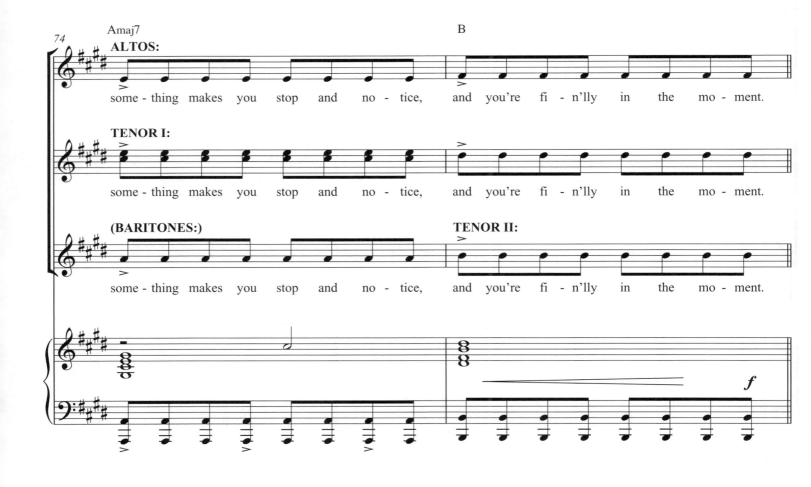

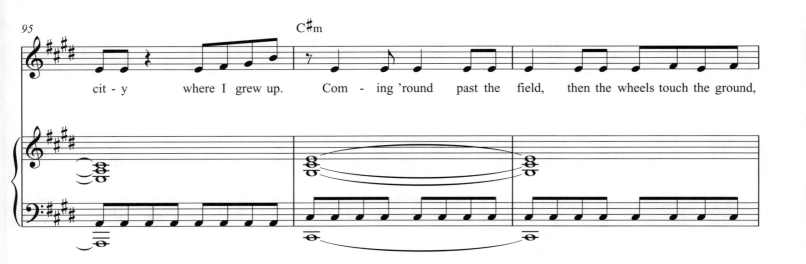

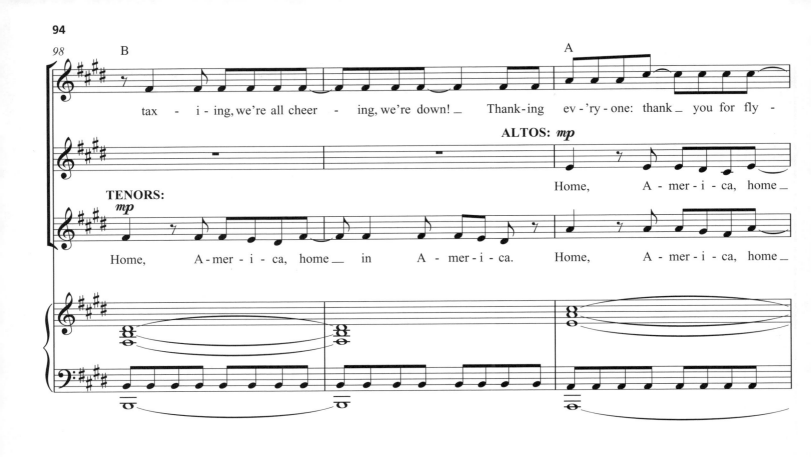

FINALE

Music and Lyrics by
IRENE SANKOFF
and DAVID HEIN

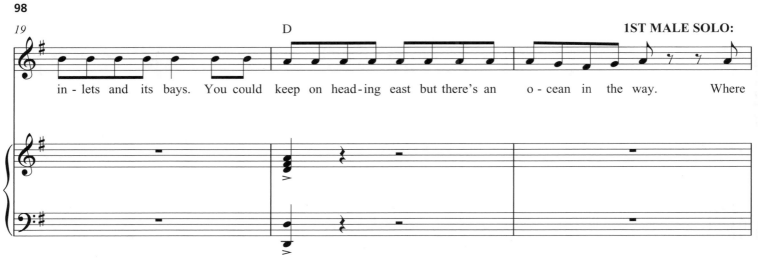

in - lets and its bays. You could keep on head-ing east but there's an o - cean in the way. Where

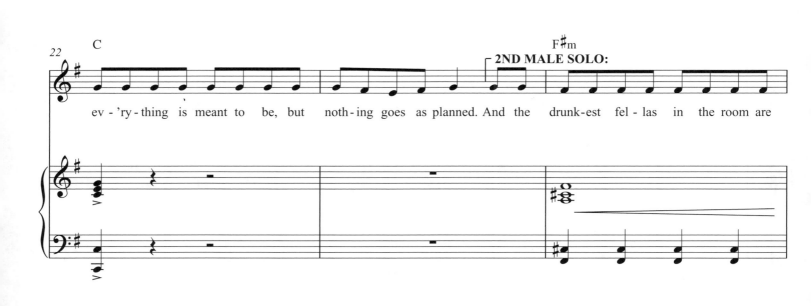

ev - 'ry-thing is meant to be, but noth-ing goes as planned. And the drunk-est fel - las in the room are

play - ing in the band.

Wel-come to the

Wel-come to the

Welcome to the fog. Welcome to the trees. A kiss, and a cod, and what-

ev-er's in be-tween. To the ones who've left, you're nev-er tru-ly gone. A

WOMEN: To the coves and the caves and the candle's in the win-dow and the

MEN: ket-tle's al-ways on. To the coves and the caves and the